THE COUNTRY CRAFT SERIES

NEEDLEPOINT

THE COUNTRY CRAFT SERIES

NEEDLEPOINT

Kate Tully

CRESCENT BOOKS
NEW YORK • AVENEL, NEW JERSEY

Previous page: Black makes a striking background to a floral arrangement.

Thanks to DMC Needlecraft Pty Ltd and Stadia Handcrafts, Sydney.
Thanks also to the Tapestry Guild of NSW.

This 1994 edition published by Crescent Books,
distributed by Outlet Book Company, Inc., a Random House Company,
40 Engelhard Avenue, Avenel, New Jersey 07001

Random House
New York • Toronto • London • Sydney • Aukland

First published in 1992
Reprinted in 1993
Reprinted in 1994

Publishing Manager: Robin Burgess
Project Coordinator: Lynn Bryan
Project assistant: Jenny Johnson
Editor: Dulcie Andrews
Illustrator: Carol Ohlbach
Photographer: Andrew Elton
Designer: Kathie Baxter Smith
Typeset in the U.K. by Seller's
Produced in Singapore by Imago

Title: Country Crafts Series: Needlepoint
ISBN: 0 517 08800 2

CONTENTS

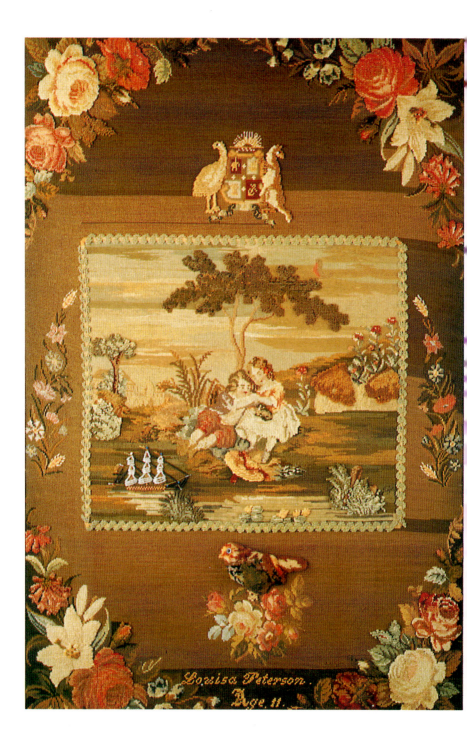

INTRODUCTION

The popularity of creating a beautiful piece of craft by hand is increasing among people of all age groups.

Through this Country Craft series, it is our hope that you will find satisfaction and enjoyment in learning a new skill. In this case, that of needlepoint, or tapestry as it is sometimes known today. We live in a hectic world and more and more people are turning to the craft. Once you have mastered the basic steps, creating your own designs for needlepoint will bring you much pleasure, as you will discover.

Opposite: This early example of Berlin wool work, incorporated in a cedar-framed fire screen, was stitched by a Louise Petersen of Queensland, Australia, in 1882 . Louise was just 11 years old when she stitched the design. Courtesy of the trustees, Museum of Applied Arts and Sciences, Sydney.

HISTORY OF NEEDLEPOINT

ORIGINALLY, THE TERM 'TAPESTRY' referred to hand-woven hangings and rugs. Such tapestries have been made since ancient Egyptian times, and during the Middle Ages they were used both to decorate and to draught-proof manors and castles. These tapestries were characterised by the richness and complexity of their designs.

Although the English word 'tapestry' was derived from the French *tapisser*, meaning 'to furnish with a rug' in modem usage needlepoint has taken on the broad meaning of an elaborate composition, a rich and decorative vision, we now talk about 'the tapestry of life' and 'the tapestry of nature'.

Just as importantly, in needlework the term has been expanded to include not just hand woven pieces but pieces worked in embroidery

Needlepoint is a rich decorating medium for today's homes. These floral pieces were designed and stitched by Janie Cooper.

titches which re-create the richness of color and design of the original tapestries and in which the design covers the whole of the background, mimicking a weaving. (In this, needlepoint differs from other types of embroidery such as cross-stitch, which leave part of the background fabric exposed.)

Needlepoint of this kind, which is the subject of this book, can also be referred to as 'tapestry', 'canvas work', 'canvas embroidery', 'evenweave embroidery', among other terms.

Both woven and embroidered needlepoints have been worked by men and women, nobility and servants, and have played some important roles in history. They have served as valuable bargaining tools and even bribes among rulers, and were vital status symbols at least until the industrial revolution.

Many early needlepoints depict historical events. The famous Bayeux Tapestry is an embroidered work illustrating the Norman Conquest of England. Others provide us with a valuable record of daily life over several centuries.

In Victorian times needlepoint became one of the most popular pastimes among society ladies. Germany produced a wide variety of ready-printed canvases and chemically dyed yarns in bright, sometimes garish colors, and these were much sought-after in Britain. The simplicity of 'Berlin woolwork', as it became known, made it easy for anyone with basic needlework skills to produce very satisfying 'fancywork' which was then transformed into decorative firescreens, footstools, cushion covers, bags, chair covers, bellpulls, slippers and any number of other items.

Today, the renaissance of needlepoint as a pastime owes as much to the Victorians' preoccupation with decoration as to the longer traditions of needlepoint drapery.

The great beauty of needlepoint as a pastime – as the Victorians found – is that its richness and complexity lie not in the technique but in the design. The technique itself could not be simpler. It takes only minutes to learn needlepoint. However, as with most things, perfection comes from practise and patience.

A relaxed attitude, in fact, is a major requirement for anyone setting out to become an accomplished needleworker. Needlepoint or, indeed, any form of needlework is not something to be hurried.

Working at needlepoint at a relaxed pace allows us to enjoy the creative process fully and helps to insure that the finished work will be even and free of mistakes.

The other requirements for working on needlepoint are a comfortable chair, good light, and some quiet time to yourself. You do not need any special space, just a bag or basket to keep your materials close at hand.

In the following chapters we will introduce you to everything you need to know to become involved in this marvelous hobby: materials and designs, techniques, methods of finishing, how to complete a 'Beginner's Project', and even tips on doing your own designing – it is easier than you think.

You can become an accomplished needlepoint worker, and discover the delights of creating something of your own using this relaxing and rewarding skill.

Spectacle cases are ideal projects for beginners. On the left are 'Irises' and 'Ottoman' designs by Nancy Kimmins; on the right, 'Lichen' design by Sarah Windrum.

TOOLS AND MATERIALS

THERE ARE TWO COMPONENTS to a piece of needlepoint–the background fabric and the thread.

The background is called the 'canvas' and this is traditionally made from cotton or linen, although other materials may be used. It must have an open, even weave so that the stitches can be uniform.

The tightness of the weave, or the 'mesh count', will determine the scale of the design, the intricacy of detail which can be worked and the thickness of thread required. For example, the finest detail can be worked on canvas with 32 threads to the inch (this work is sometimes called *petit point*). Mesh counts are still most commonly given in threads per inch, although some suppliers have adopted a metric system of threads per 10cm. A 'mesh' is 'an intersection of vertical and horizontal threads'. Work will proceed faster on 7-mesh canvas, but it will have less detail and it will require thicker yarn, while rugs are worked on 3-mesh canvas.

There are three types of canvas commonly used for needlepoint: single, interlocked and double (sometimes called 'Penelope').

18-mesh interlocked canvas worked with two strands of crewel wool.

7-mesh double canvas worked with two strands of needlepoint wool.

10-mesh double ('Penelope') canvas worked with three strands of Persian wool, with petit point detail worked in one strand of Persian.

Single (mono) is usually used for fine work it comes in the highest mesh counts (although some stitchers prefer to use double canvas and split the twin threads in areas where more detail is required). However, single canvas is woven in the simplest way and, in its lower mesh counts, some stitchers find it unstable and difficult to work. It is usually stiffer than the other types of canvas.

Interlocked is a form of single canvas where the horizontal thread separates and interlocks at each mesh, giving extra stability. This canvas tends to distort less than the others during working.

Double (Penelope) is usually more pliable than single or interlocked, as two finer threads are used to provide the same strength as the single threads of the other varieties. In some double canvas, the twin threads one way are closer together than the other two; the closer threads should run vertically through the work.

Most canvases are either white, preferred for work where the predominant colors are light, or a natural, 'antique' finish which is better under dark work.

Non-traditional canvases include plastic canvas for such items as placemats and boxes, and 'waste' or 'breakaway' canvas. The latter is used to apply a design to another fabric, with more applications in cross-stitch and forms of embroidery than in needlepoint.

As our aim in needlepoint is to cover the canvas almost completely, you need to know which canvas you will be using before you select the threads to be used.

Most needlepoint is worked in one of three types of wool – crewel, Persian, or needlepoint. These are purpose designed, with long fibers giving the strength required when a piece of yarn will be passed repeatedly through the coarse canvas. Most brands are now colorfast and mothproof.

Crewel is a finely textured two-ply thread used singly for very fine work, or in multiple threads on canvases with lower mesh counts.

Persian is a loosely twisted three-ply wool in which the strands can be easily separated. This makes it a most versatile yarn in several ways. Firstly, if a strand of Persian is not quite sufficient to cover the canvas, its plies can be separated and then retwisted more loosely, effectively thickening the strand. Secondly, it is ideal for blending.

For example, if one strand of needlepoint wool will not cover the canvas, but a double strand is too thick, one or two strands of Persian can be added to the single needlepoint strand. The Persian can be in the same color as the needlepoint wool, or in another shade for extra visual interest.

Needlepoint is a tightly twisted four-ply yarn which is generally used as a single or double thread. It has the smooth appearance of worsted knitting wool and it gives an attractive, even finish. It is not designed to be separated; if it is, the smoothness is lost.

Although these three wools are the most common threads for needlepoint, virtually any thread can be used as long as it is compatible with the canvas. This means that it must be thick enough to cover the canvas, but not so thick as to distort the holes as it passes through.

Some examples of other suitable threads are homespun wool, angora, embroidery cottons (available in mat, low-sheen and glossy finishes) and metallic threads, or a combination of any threads (see photograph)

Some synthetic threads can stretch and pill (form small balls of fiber), so they are not suitable, and some knitting wools are too soft and will break during use.

If in doubt about a thread's suitability, try it on a small section of canvas. Threads that are not designed for needlepoint should be used in short lengths – not more than 12 inches at a time.

Items such as beads, buttons, and ribbons can also be successfully incorporated into needlepoint work.

Apart from the canvas and thread, you will need a few simple tools.

Needlepoint needles are blunt so there is less danger of splitting the canvas or threads, and they have large eyes to take the wool.

When the needle is threaded, it should pass through the holes in the canvas without distorting them. Using a needle of the correct size for your wool and canvas will help prevent tangling and excessive wear of your wool (see

THE RIGHT WOOL			
Mesh count of canvas	Strands of yarn for tent stitch		
	crewel*	Persian *	needlepoint*
18	2	1	–
14	3	2	–
12	4	2	1
10	5	3	1
7	8	6	2

* Remember that crewel has two strands in one thread, Persian has three. Needlepoint wool is non-divisible, therefore each thread counts as a single strand.

THE RIGHT NEEDLE	
Mesh count of canvas	Needle size
3 to 8	14 to 16
10 to 14	18 to 20
16 to 24	22 to 24

A selection of yarns suitable for needlepoint, (clockwise from top) cre

ol, hanks and skeins of needlepoint wool and mat embroidery cottons.

lap frame with canvas

embroidery
scissors

fingertip
guard

thimble

dressmaking scissors

18

table below).

Two pairs of scissors are needed: fine pointed embroidery scissors to pick out the threads to be cut, and dressmaking or household scissors to cut the canvas. Embroidery scissors should not be used for this purpose.

A thimble is a matter of choice, but using one can make your work easier in the long term. Or use a leather fingertip guard.

The other important item of equipment for needlepoint is a frame. Anyone who has not used one before may find a frame awkward to start with, but you should persevere. Work done on a frame can proceed quickly and evenly. Frames are discussed in more detail in the following chapter.

Beyond these basic requirements there is a remarkable array of aids and accessories which are intended to make the stitcher's work easier. These things are available at any needlework store and they include such items as thread organizers, chart markers and a hands-free magnifying glass.

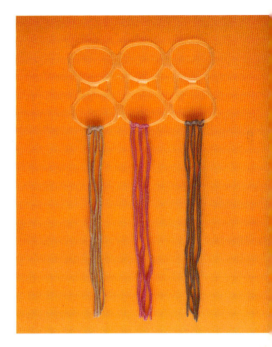

The plastic rings from a six-pack of cans make an ideal thread organizer.

Opposite: The basic needlepoint crafts kit.

A beautiful country house scene stitched in wool, in long stitch.
The oval wooden frame completes the picture.

STARTING WORK

CHOOSING YOUR FIRST PROJECT is enjoyable, yet it should not be taken too lightly. It is very important to choose something that you will like and will use when you have finished it. If you are too ambitious you may become discouraged and give up.

The easiest way to get started is with a kit, where all the big decisions have been made for you. A kit will contain the canvas with a ready-printed design, the correct quantity of wool in the designated colors and of the correct weight, and the right needle.

Many advanced stitchers regard kits with some disdain, yet millions of people have been introduced to the delights of needlepoint in this way. Small kits are an inexpensive way to try out your new knowledge and the results can be very satisfying. Larger, more complex kits are also available and feature some very attractive designs, both traditional and contemporary.

When they want something more challenging than a small beginner's kit, many stitchers progress to a larger canvas which also has the design printed on, or possibly 'trammed'. Tramming uses long stitches to show which wools are to be used by the stitcher.

Tramming may be used with or instead of printed designs. Trammed canvases are generally more expensive than printed ones, but they require less wool as the needlepoint can be worked in half cross-stitch (see 'Techniques of the Craft').

Some canvases also have areas of fine detail, such as faces and hands, already worked in *petit point*. Others are available in one-off, hand-painted designs.

When you are looking at printed or painted canvases remember that the colors used are seldom those of the recommended wools. The canvas colors must be brighter and show more contrast to make it easier for the stitcher to know which color to use where. The color key at the side of the canvas will indicate the exact wools recommended, so you need to look at these when deciding whether you like the piece. If quantities are not given, ask the store staff for guidance.

Canvases which are sold on their own allow more scope for individuality than kits because you can vary the colors to suit your taste. For example, if a motif uses three tones of blue, you could replace these with three tones of pink, purple, yellow or whatever you like. Be sure that the thread will completely cover the canvas background.

With printed, painted and most trammed canvases, you are also free to choose the background color.

As a rule, designs requiring more colors will be more complicated to work because you will start and finish threads more often, and you will possibly have many small areas of shading.

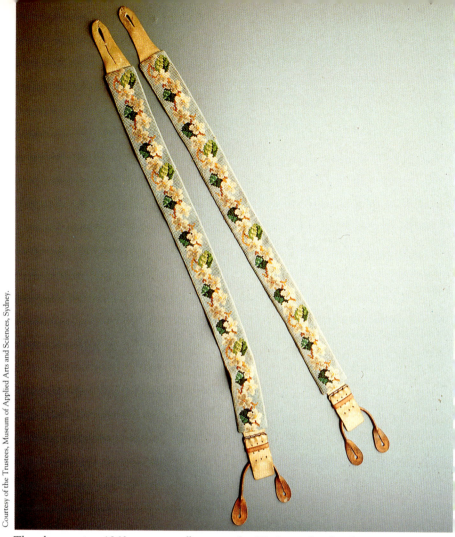

These braces, circa 1860, are an excellent example of Berlin woolwork. They are embroidered in a cross-stitch floral design in tones of yellow, cream and brown on a pale blue background.

Besides kits and the various prepared canvases, you can start a needlepoint with a blank canvas and a chart. It is unfortunate that charts are not as varied for needlepoint as they are for other forms of needlework, most notably cross-stitch. Stitchers wanting more of a challenge can 'grow out of' what they regard as the paint-by-numbers nature of kits and prepared canvases and they find their options in charts relatively limited.

However, there is now a fast-growing number of beautiful needlepoint charts available in books and brochures. This is a recognition of the revival of interest in needlepoint as a needlework form. Also, charts for cross-stitch and other stitching techniques are easily adapted for needlepoint and these should never be disregarded.

Finally, as you will discover in the 'Beginner's Project', making your own charts is easier than you might think.

When buying a large quantity of one color thread, such as the background color, be sure that each skein has the same dye lot number. It is sometimes possible to buy background wool in large hanks, which are more economical than the smaller skeins.

Remember to ask at the store about washing or dry cleaning the thread if there is no advice on the label.

Some threads come pre-cut into lengths ready to use, others are in a continuous skein. Having them pre-cut means you will not use threads which are too long.

If your threads are not pre-cut, take the time to prepare them before you start work. Cut each skein into lengths no greater than 18 inches. Some skeins are wound in such a way that you simply untwist them and cut through one end of the loop. Tie each color together in a loose knot, or attach these to a commercial or home-made thread organizer. The plastic rings from a six-pack of aluminum cans are ideal.

Always buy good quality canvas with no irregularities. Allow 2 inches more than the design area on all sides.

If you are working from a chart onto blank canvas, use either an indelible pen (not a pencil) or basting stitches to mark in the margins of your work, taking the number of meshes from the number of squares on your chart. If the piece is small, you can mark just the center lines for reference (mark these on the chart too, if they are not there already). On a larger canvas, it is preferable to mark in the whole grid system (usually squares). This will make it much easier to follow the chart.

Leave the canvas as a square or rectangle, even if the finished item will be another shape. This way it will be simpler to mount on a frame and it will be easier to block (see 'Finishing Techniques').

Place the canvas on a piece of paper and in indelible ink trace the outline of the finished design area. You will use this template (pattern) when blocking the work.

Of needlepoint frames, traditionalists will say that any piece of canvas more than 8 inches square should be mounted on a frame for working. Contemporary experts with a more liberal attitude claim that frames 'cramp their style'.

As we have already said, anyone working with a frame for the first few times will feel clumsy and constricted. However, with practise, anyone can manage it and you will discover that there are real advantages.

Working with a frame forces you to use the two-movement, poking technique, passing the needle to the back of the work with one hand and then through to the front from underneath, usually with the other hand. This gives the stitcher more control over the work and thus produces a more even finish.

The other technique, the single movement 'scooping' is harder on the thread, produces less even tension and also creates more distortion in the canvas. Scooping is impossible when the work is on a frame because the canvas is too taut.

Needlepoint worked without a frame will almost always require blocking when it is completed, whereas a frame sometimes alleviates the need for this process.

The illustrations show how canvas is mounted on a frame.

A sheet of clear, self-adhesive plastic over your chart helps protect it from wear and tear, spilt coffee, and the chart is easier to roll .

MOUNTING A NEEDLEPOINT ON A FRAME

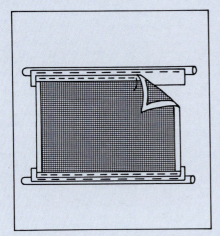

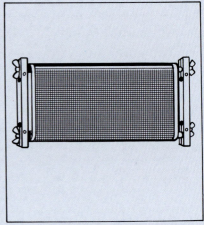

Rotating frame

Most popular needlepoint frames are rectangular and follow the same principles to keep the canvas as square as possible. Frames are traditionally made from timber, although newer designs use plastic tubing.

Frames where all sides are fixed are called 'slates'; those with adjustable scrolls at top and bottom are called 'rotating frames'.

Smaller frames are held on the lap and steadied with one hand against a table, the end of a sofa or any appropriate surface. Larger frames have their own stands, leaving both hands free to manipulate the needle.

Before mounting canvas on a frame, bind the sides with masking tape. This will stop the thread from snagging, which is detrimental both to the thread and to the stitcher's patience. (If no frame is being used, all edges should be bound in this way.)

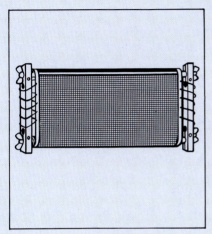
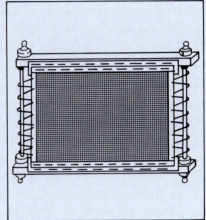

Slate frame

Fold over 1 inch at the top and bottom of the canvas, center along the tapes on the scrolls or battens and baste in place with strong thread.

Screw the two side battens in place on either end of the bottom piece. Wind the top scroll of a rotating frame, or adjust the side battens on a fixed slate frame, to make the canvas as taut as possible, before screwing all pieces of the frame together.

Lace the sides of the canvas to the battens. If you are using a rotating frame, this lacing will need to be undone and replaced as the work is wound up in scrolls.

TECHNIQUES OF THE CRAFT

THE BEST WAY TO LEARN any new skill is simply to do it. Do not be afraid to start on a project lest you make mistakes. In needlepoint, there is no right or wrong way. The techniques we use today are those which our predecessors found did the job best, but there is always room for experimentation and individuality.

If your design features a major motif on a plain background, it is best to work the motif first and the background last. Working in sections of one color at a time, work either from the top to the bottom or from the center outward, depending on the design.

If the design includes both diagonal tent stitches and straight stitches, work the tent stitches first.

If you are working from a chart in one of the traditional tent stitches (see boxed section), each square on the chart represents one stitch over one mesh (where a vertical thread intersects a horizontal thread). In working a row of stitches, say six stitches for example, you can choose to count either six threads or six holes on the canvas. The result will be the same, as long as you are consistent.

Remember that each square on the chart represents a stitch, regardless of the mesh count of the canvas. Thus 30 stitches will cover less than one inch on 32-mesh canvas, while the same 30 stitches from the same

chart will cover three inches on 10-mesh canvas.

Stitches of different colors will be indicated on charts either by symbols or by colors, often exaggerated (as on printed canvases) to make them easier to distinguish.

The finished work will look different from the chart, as squares are translated into sloping stitches. This difference is particularly noticeable on diagonal lines and curves, as shown in the illustrations. (These shapes also highlight the detail achievable on canvases of different mesh counts).

If the stitches on the chart give you an effect you are not pleased with, experiment by blending strands of different colors into the one thread to achieve a more pleasing effect.

When working on printed canvas, too, you can be uncertain which colors to use for which stitches, especially in places where one color meets another. Be flexible and try several alternatives until you are happy.

To start stitching, take a thread no longer than 18 inches. Longer threads will tangle and slow you down and the end of the yarn will be thinner and more worn than the beginning. Pull the thread 6 inches through your needle. You will move the needle closer to the end of the thread as you work.

If you are working in tent stitch, tie a loose

Opposite: This country scene is stitched in basic half cross-stitch on a prepared French canvas.

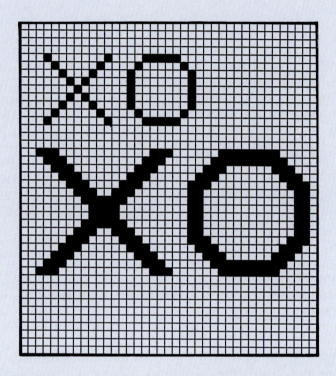

Designs which appear uniform on the square grid of a chart (see above) will look different when worked in diagonal tent stitches. If you look closely at the photographs on the opposite page, you will see that using a finer mesh (below right) and thread allows a greater detail to be worked. Both are the same design, but the resultant effect is different.

STITCH GUIDE

There are dozens of stitches which can be used for needlepoint, but they can be divided into two main types: small diagonal stitches called 'tent' stitches which are common in traditional work, and straight stitches which are found in myriad forms in more contemporary stitching.

Tent   All tent stitches look the same from the front, being worked across a single mesh. Their suitability for different projects is determined by the pattern of stitches created at the back of the work.

Straight   Straight stitches can be worked vertically, horizontally and diagonally over any number of meshes. They are used to create textural effects and also to fill in a background faster than tent stitches. Tension is very important to insure that the canvas is fully covered.
Straight stitches can be used in random lengths, in repetitive patterns such as Bargello (also called Florentine work), and to create individual, ornamental stitches (see illustrations).

Continental   An easy stitch which has long, sloping threads at the back, making a good backing for cushions and small upholstered items. It has a natural diagonal pull so it is best worked on a frame. It can be worked vertically (top to bottom) or horizontally (right to left); the work should be turned at end of each row.

Basketweave   Biases less than Continental stitch and gives an excellent, hard-wearing backing, making it the preferred stitch for larger upholstered items. It is worked in diagonals from top right of work to bottom left. Continental can be worked in areas where detail is too fine for basketweave.

Half cross   Produces small, straight stitches at the back of the work, making a weak backing which is suitable mostly for framed needlepoints or other work which will not be subjected to wear. Worked on trammed and double canvas only, half cross does not adequately cover single canvas. It is worked from left to right.

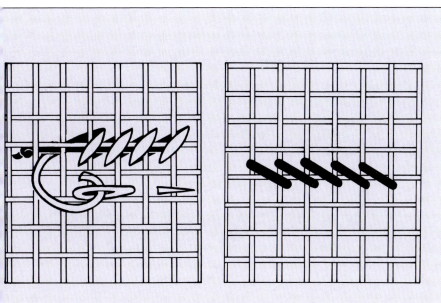

Starting the first thread – tent stitch

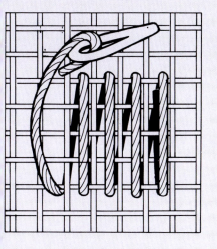

Starting the first thread – straight stitch

Starting subsequent threads and finishing – straight stitch

STITCH GUIDE

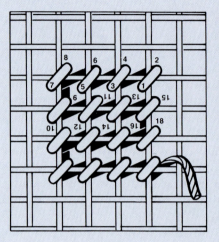
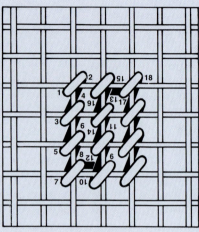

Continental stitch

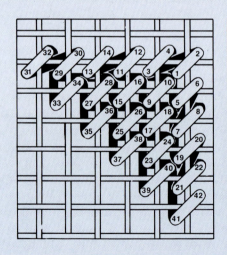
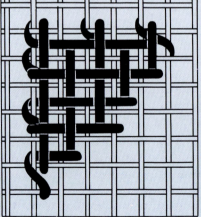

Basketweave stitch (left) and reverse of the stitch (right)

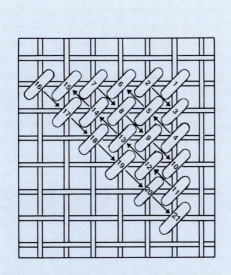

Basketweave: sequence of stitches

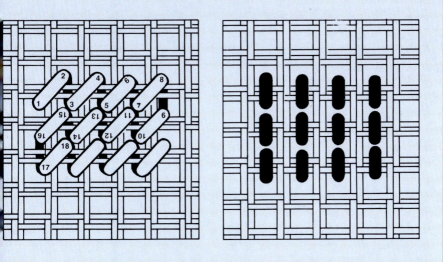

Horizontal half cross-stitch and reverse of the stitch

STITCH GUIDE

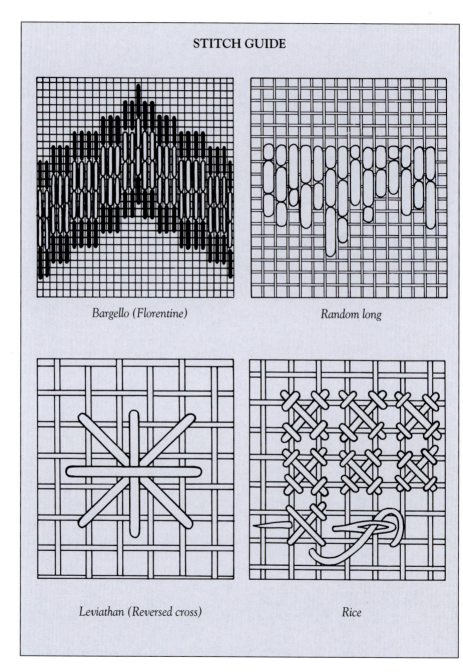

Bargello (Florentine)

Random long

Leviathan (Reversed cross)

Rice

knot in the end of the thread and pass it through the canvas from the right side, about 1 inch from where you will start work. Work the first few stitches over the thread at the back of the work and cut off the knot when you come to it.

For straight stitches, weave the thread through the canvas for 1 inch.

Subsequent threads for either type of stitch can be started by weaving through the back of existing stitches in two directions. Threads are finished in the same way (see illustrations).

Do not scrimp on the thread used for starting and finishing – it is far more difficult to darn a thread back in if it comes loose than to secure it properly in the first place.

Try not to start and finish a lot of threads in the same place, as lumps will appear.

Where possible, threads should be started and finished in stitches of the same or a similar color, or there is a danger that they will show through.

Similarly, threads can be carried across the back of the work for about 1 inch by working into existing stitches, or by crossing a section that will later be stitched, but again the colors need to tone, or carried threads will be apparent from the right side.

Tension can vary slightly from one stitcher to another, but the work must be even and cover the canvas fully without being sloppy (see photograph).

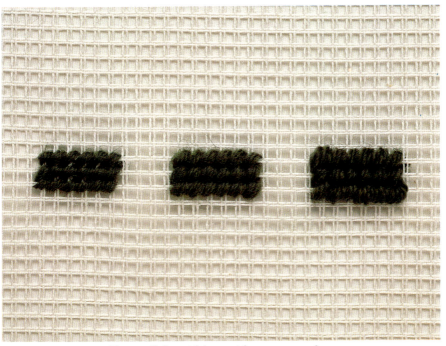

Tension (left to right): too tight, correct, too loose.

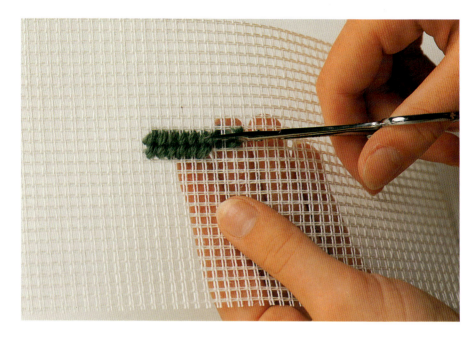

Cutting out stitches.

Some twisting in your threads is normal during work, although if they twist constantly, you are using threads which are too long. When twisting occurs, allow the thread to dangle from the work and untwist itself. If you have already worked a few stitches with the thread tightly twisted, these stitches will probably not cover the canvas properly and should be gently undone (do not pull) and reworked when the thread is untwisted.

If you have to undo more than a few stitches, you should not reuse the thread but finish it off and start a new one. The thread which has been unpicked will be worn and its stitches will look different.

Where large sections need to be undone because of a problem with the thread or a mistake, it is best to cut out the stitches. Unpicking a large section can distort the canvas and make the reworked stitches uneven. To cut out stitches, use your fine pointed embroidery scissors to snip carefully through each stitch from the right side, then pull out the stitches from the wrong side, using your finger tips or tweezers.

If you break the wool during stitching, undo stitches far enough to darn in the end of the thread and start a new one.

A problem which you should take every care to avoid, but which happens occasionally, is a cut in the canvas. If this does occur, cut a small patch from the same canvas, baste it to the wrong side of the work and stitch that area through both thicknesses, then remove basting.

If you are not using a frame, try to roll the canvas rather than crumple it to reach the area you are working on. Rolls can be held in place with large safety pins.

It is preferable to store your work in a natural cloth bag, rather than a plastic one. In humid conditions there is always a danger of needles rusting and leaving marks or stains on your work.

Patching canvas.

FINISHING TECHNIQUES

MANY NEEDLEPOINT pieces are distorted whilst being worked especially pieces worked without a frame and pieces worked predominantly in Continental stitch. Blocking is required to return them to the correct shape. Some picture-framers will block a needlepoint for you, but you can do it yourself. (see page 40).

If blocking is not required, small corrections to shape can be made using a steam iron.

The top pin cushion is stitched in a straight stitch design while the bottom one is worked in tent stitch and embellished with French knots.

Place the needlepoint face-down on a folded towel on the ironing board, cover it with a damp cloth and iron it lightly until it is dry, pulling it gently into shape.

If your needlepoint needs cleaning at any stage, there are two alternatives. You can have it dry cleaned if you know your threads and canvas are dry-cleanable, or you can hand wash it. Try first to sponge out marks using a tiny amount of mild soap. Sponge lightly taking care not to rub the work as the threads will fluff and pill (form small balls of fluff).

Hand washing is best done in the tub or shower where the work can be laid flat. Use a small amount of mild soap in cool to tepid water – too much soap will wash out the sizing from the canvas, making it limp. Press the work from the back with a sponge. Rinse it several times. Do not wring. Re-block.

If you choose dry cleaning, go to a dry cleaner you trust. Your local needlework store maybe able to recommend a dry cleaner in your area. Make sure the needlepoint is not pressed or the textural appeal will be minimal. Press the work lightly yourself, using a damp cloth, as above.

Where the work is to be made into a

HALF CROSS-STITCH JOIN

FOLDLINE
1.5cm

Half cross-stitch can be used to make an invisible join in the same color as the stitching, or a decorative seam if a contrasting thread is chosen.

Trim the seam allowance to 3/8 inch and fold over along the first canvas thread after the work (not through a line of holes). Thread a blunt-ended needlepoint needle and secure the thread in the back of the stitches at the bottom of the right hand piece.

With right sides facing you and the work lined up exactly, bring the needle up through the bottom left-hand hole then into the right-hand hole, one row above. Bring it up again in the next left-hand hole, thus creating a half cross-stitch. Continue in this manner up the seam, then fasten off the thread.

cushion or is to be used for upholstery, some stitchers work two rows of 'sacrifice stitches' (extra) all around the edge. These stitches are then enclosed in the seam or behind upholstery braid, giving the cover extra strength.

It is preferable to make up items such as cushions and bags by hand-sewn back stitch rather than by machine. In this way you can pass the needle through holes in the canvas and between stitches, whereas a machine needle will split the threads and possibly split the canvas all along the seam where you most need strength.

Where two pieces of needlepoint are to be joined, use either half cross-stitch for an invisible join, or binding stitch for a decorative edging. Both these stitches are illustrated.

BLOCKING A NEEDLEPOINT

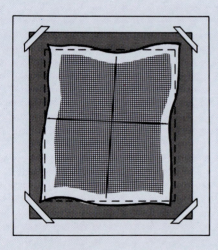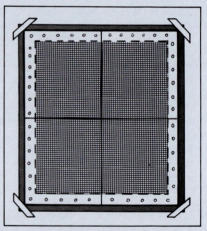

Place your template upside-down on a piece of clean wood and lay the needlepoint face-down on top of it. Dampen the work thoroughly with water, using a spray or sponge.

Using rustproof tacks, pins or small nails, tack the needlepoint into shape, using the template as a guide. Fix it first in the center of each side, then work out towards the corners.

Allow to dry completely, which may take several days. Insure the needlepoint is not in a damp place, or it may become musty and even attract mildew.

You might choose to paint the back of the work with a clear-drying wallpaper paste which will help to hold the work in shape after blocking. Ask your needlework suppliers to recommend a brand. Allow the paste to dry completely before removing the needlepoint from the block.

BINDING STITCH JOIN

This is a decorative seam which can be used to join two pieces of needlepoint and to form a braided edging on a single piece. Trim the seam allowances to 3/8 inch. The binding stitch is worked over two threads, so on double canvas fold along a twin thread, but on single fold along a row of holes and include two threads in the stitch.

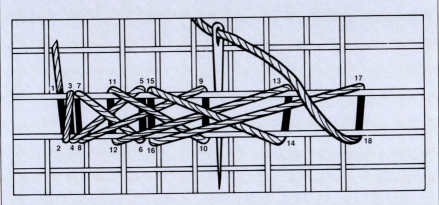

Thread a blunt-ended needlepoint needle and secure the thread in the back of the edge stitches. Working from left to right, follow the sequence of stitches indicated in the diagram, matching mesh for mesh. Fasten off thread in the back of the needlepoint.

BEGINNER'S PROJECT

IN THIS PROJECT we will take you right from the design process through to the finished article, a pin cushion. You will see that coming up with your own designs is not as difficult as you might think.

Designing should be a creative pleasure for you. There are plenty of books to advise on color, form and design elements, so here we will concentrate on the process of translating a pictorial reference into a needlepoint chart.

Your reference might be a photograph, a page from a magazine or a book, a painting, gift-wrap, notepaper, wallpaper, fabric or, indeed, any type of picture. This exercise uses as references an illustration of an apple from a horticultural textbook for the central design (Figs. 1a and 1b) and a piece of gingham fabric for the border.

Start the design process by choosing the appropriate canvas of 12-mesh to give the required detail.

Decide on the approximate size for the finished work: 5 inches square. On 12-mesh canvas this means 60 stitches by 60 stitches (5 inches] x 12 stitches = 60 stitches).

On a piece of graph paper you would then mark the outline of 60 x 60 squares and draw in the area to be occupied by the border. Then you would sketch the apple into the space in the middle of the chart and gradually refine its outline to your satisfaction (Fig. 3).

To simplify the design for stitching, we made the apple a single red and the stem a

Fig. 1a

Fig 1 b. From The Oxford Book of Food Plants © Oxford University Press 1975 Reproduced by permission.

single brown, and reduced the shading in the leaves to a light and mid-green. The lines of major shading determined where each green was used.

With the addition of the border, using the gingham fabric as a reference, the final design is 58 x 58 stitches (Fig. 4).

Apart from this method, you can also transfer a reference to a chart by using a transparent grid overlay. These are commercially available or you can make your own by photocopying graph paper onto tracing paper or onto the plastic sheets used with overhead projectors.

The transparent grid is laid over the reference and you can see immediately which square (and therefore which stitch) is which color (Fig. 2).

The scale of the grid with the choice of canvas determines the intricacy of detail possible and the size of the finished design. For example, if you have chosen 12-mesh canvas, every 12 squares on the grid will translate into 1 inch of stitching. Therefore, if you want a motif such as our apple to be around 2 inches wide, you will need to use a grid which fits around 24 squares across the motif.

Fig. 2.

Fig. 3.

As you become more confident in your designing, you can prepare a chart without any references. Simply mark up the graph paper to size as already described, depending on your choice of canvas and the desired size of the finished work, then sketch or paint on your own design. Eventually you may even gain sufficient confidence to paint your design directly onto the canvas.

The information in this book will help you to choose the correct canvas and thread for any project you design. Remember to buy the canvas at least 2 inches larger all round than the finished design.

It can be tricky to gauge the amount of thread required, but your local needlework store can advise you. As a rough guide, 10-mesh to 14-mesh canvas will take

Fig. 4.

approximately 7 inches of wool when using Continental or basketweave stitch, or 4 1/4 inches in half cross or straight stitch for every square 1/2 inch to be covered.

MATERIALS REQUIRED

Needlepoint wool in the following colors and skein quantities:

red x 1	light green x 1
brown x 1	mid green x 1
ecru x 2	dark green x 1

- 12-mesh interlock canvas, 8 x 8 inches
- Backing fabric, 8 x 8 inches
- Batting
- Strong sewing thread
- Needlepoint needle
- Crewel needle

INSTRUCTIONS

Bind edges of canvas with masking tape. With indelible pen, mark in outline 58 x 58 stitches. Take a template of design area.

As this piece is small, it can be worked in the hand, without a frame. Stitch the apple in basketweave. Then work the leaves and stem in Continental, turning the work at the end of each row. (These sections are too small for basketweave.)

Next, fill in the background in basketweave and finally work the border in Continental. The centers of the gingham border (in ecru) could even be worked in half cross-stitch over the padding provided by the greens.

Using your template, block the finished work. Place it face-down on the backing fabric and baste it in place. Using strong sewing thread and your crewel needle, backstitch the two pieces together along the top and sides. Trim the seams to 3/8 inch and cut across the corners. Turn right side out and fill with batting, paying particular attention to the corners. Turn under the bottom seam allowance of the canvas and backing fabric and stitch in place.

Make a twisted cord as follows: cut 3 5/8 yards of your remaining red wool and fold it in three. Secure one end of the 'loop' (around a small door knob, for example) and twist the three strands together a hundred times. Bring the two ends together and knot them immediately. The rest of the loop will twist itself into a cord.

Stitch the cord around the seam, overlapping it at the knot and stitching it in place to neaten.

INDEX